A LOVE JOUR

100 Things
I about
DAD

Jeff Bogle

ROCKRIDGE
PRESS

Series Designer: Liz Cosgrove
Interior and Cover Designer: Lindsey Decker
Art Producer: Janice Ackerman
Editor: Adrian Potts
Production Editor: Matthew Burnett
Production Manager: Jose Olivera

Cover Illustration: Bibadash/shutterstock.com.
Interior Illustration: Courtesy of shutterstock.com.

Paperback ISBN: 978-1-63807-335-2
R0

From:

To:

with lots of love

Date:

Author's Note

Having had a great dad and being the proud papa of two remarkable young ladies myself, I understand that sometimes it's difficult to say which is better: being a dad to wonderful children or having had the privilege of being raised by a fantastic father. Thankfully, this journal will encourage reflection on both fronts!

You'll be asked to think about not only the lessons your dad has taught, examples set, jokes made, vacations taken, and passions shared with you. But you will also reflect on the traits you two have in common, and the ways you have actually helped to make each other's lives richer and more memorable. There are also "extra love" pages throughout that provide room for additional sweet memories, like more details, pictures, or other mementos.

My hope is that by having fun answering these prompts, making many awesome top three lists, and reflecting back on the best of times shared together, you will appreciate even further the special relationship you've enjoyed with your dad.

With much love,
to you and your dad!
Jeff

1.

I'm happy that I got my

.... from you.

2.

Your

. . . .

inspires me.

3.

I love how dedicated you are

to ....

"extra love"

4.

You show me that you love me when

you ....

and ....

5.

I love that you're always learning, including

....

and ....

6.

The best game we play together

is ....

7.

The top three things you've given me

that I'll always keep with me are . . .

1. ....

2. ....

3. ....

8.

Someday, I hope to be as good of

a(n) .... as you are.

9.

WHEN I WAS LITTLE, I LOVED WHEN
YOU WOULD READ ....
AND .... TO ME.

10.

If there was a movie made about us,
the actor .... would
play you, and my part would be played
by ....

11.

Because of you, Dad, I was able

to ....

12.

I appreciate the way you love the small things

in life, like .... and

....

13.

The top three life lessons

you have taught me are . . .

1. ....

2. ....

3. ....

14.

When I was younger, I loved to

.... with you.

15.

I love that we both like

to ....

16.

You've taught me a lot, but the most
important thing I've learned from you is
how to ....

17.

.... has always been

my favorite place to spend time together.

18.

My perfect day with you involves

.... ,

.... , and

....

19.

You make me laugh every single time you

say (or do) ....

20.

....

is a movie we love to rewatch together

because ....

21.

Your favorite thing about me is my

....

22.

My favorite thing about you is your

....

23.

I'll never forget when you

.... for me.

24.

The top three most memorable

places you've taken me are . . .

1. ....

2. ....

3. ....

25.

I love that no matter how busy you are, you always find time to ....

26.

Sometimes you get frustrated when

I .... ,

but I always know that you still love me.

27.

You know how to

....

better than anyone I know.

28.

Thanks to you, I had the courage

to ....

"extra love"

29.

Of the gifts I have given you, I hope you

keep .... forever.

30.

Of all the things you've given me,

I cherish .... and

.... the most.

31.

I HAVE NEVER BEEN PROUDER TO BE
YOUR CHILD THAN WHEN I SAW
YOU ....

32.

When I need advice about ....,

you always have something wise to say,

like ....

33.

The top three dad jokes you tell are . . .

1. ....

2. ....

3. ....

34.

If you were a flavor of ice cream, you'd

be .... because you're

.... and ....

35.

You act tough, but .... always

makes you cry, and I love that about you!

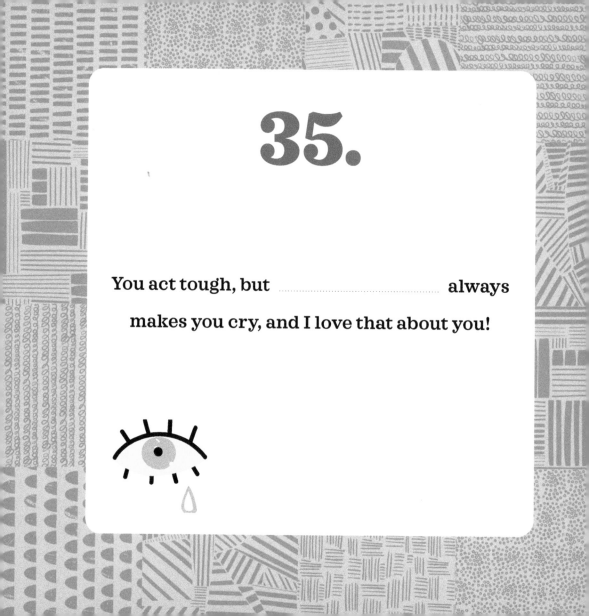

36.

I wouldn't be the person I am today without

your ....

37.

If you could travel anywhere, it would be

to ....

38.

I love it when you wear your favorite

. . . .

39.

I love hearing your stories about

....

and ....

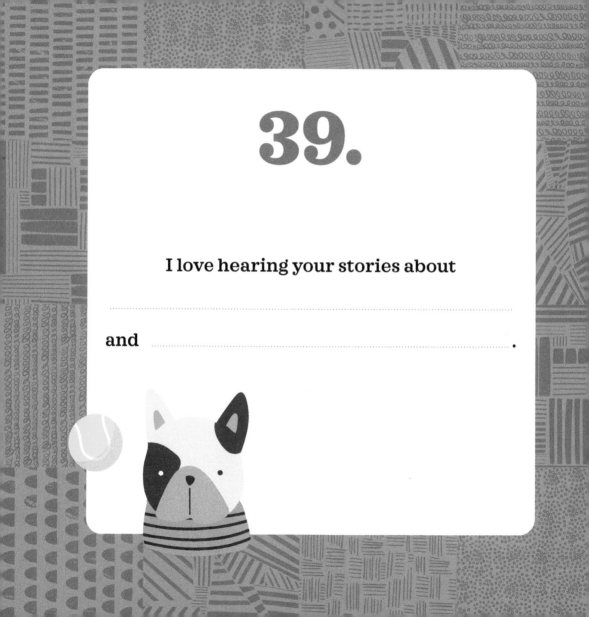

40.

The top three old-fashioned things

you do that I love are . . .

1. ....

2. ....

3. ....

41.

If you were an animal, you would be

a .... because

you .... and ....

42.

Your nickname for me is

....,

which I love!

43.

My friends think you're cool because
you _____ .

44.

I think you are cool because you

....

45.

I WAS PROUD TO WATCH YOU ACHIEVE

YOUR DREAM OF ....

46.

"   "

is something you say a lot, but

I never get tired of hearing it.

47.

You taught me to appreciate

....

and ....

48.

.... is something

you do, not because you love it,

but because it makes me happy.

49.

I learned how to ....

by watching you do it well and with passion.

50.

Your superpower as a dad is ....

....

51.

The top three words that

remind me of you are . . .

1. ....

2. ....

3. ....

52.

Because of you, I know how important

.... is,

and this knowledge has changed my life.

53.

I get my love of .... and

.... from you.

"extra love"

54.

THE HAPPIEST I'VE EVER SEEN YOU IS
WHEN YOU WERE ....

55.

By watching the way you ....

and ...., you've taught me

the importance of having a positive attitude.

56.

I love that you never ....

57.

You love it when I ....

58.

It's one of the quirkiest things about you,

but I love the way you ....

59.

The top three things I love that

we do together are . . .

1. ....

2. ....

3. ....

60.

The way you ....

always makes me smile.

61.

You helped me realize a dream of mine

when you ....

62.

I WAS SAD WHEN ....,

BUT YOU CHEERED ME UP BY

....

63.

You introduced me to the music of

...., and I still love it!

64.

You're a great dad, but you were there for me

as a friend when I ....

65.

I love it when we cook/bake ....,

....,

and .... together.

66.

MY FAVORITE DAY WITH YOU, THE ONE
I WISH WE COULD RELIVE OVER AND OVER
AGAIN, IS ....

67.

The top three traits we have in common are . . .

1. ....

2. ....

3. ....

68.

The best gift you've given me was

....

69.

YOU HELPED ME OVERCOME MY FEAR OF

....

WHEN YOU ....

70.

Under the word ....

in the dictionary, there should be a

picture of you.

71.

The topic I could listen to you talk

passionately about forever is

....

72.

I admire the way you

....

73.

You're not the only one who teaches!

You love that I helped you learn how to

....

74.

....

is my favorite thing about you, Dad.

75.

I love that you lead by example. I learned to

.... by watching the

way you ....

76.

You work so hard. I love that you relax on days off by ....

"extra love"

77.

I think it's cool that you collect

....

78.

.... WAS

THE SCENE OF OUR GREATEST ADVENTURE!

79.

I didn't understand it right away,

but I'm so happy you taught me about

.... **and** ....

80.

I LOVE THE WAY YOU ROOT FOR ME.
MY FAVORITE TIME YOU CHEERED
ME ON WAS WHILE I ....

81.

The top three awards you should win
(in addition to Best Dad Ever!) are . . .

1. ....

2. ....

3. ....

82.

I'LL ALWAYS REMEMBER HOW YOU
CAME TO MY RESCUE AND SAVED THE DAY
WHEN I ....

83.

.... is a secret between us

that we promised to never tell!

84.

.... is the silliest thing

I ever saw you do, and I'll never forget it!

85.

I'LL ALWAYS REMEMBER THAT SUMMER
WHEN WE ....

86.

You always believe in me, even when my ideas

are a little wacky, like the time I wanted to

....

87.

Sometimes I groan, but I secretly love it when you ....

88.

MY FAVORITE HOLIDAY MEMORY IS WHEN

WE ....

89.

I'm so grateful that you shared your passions

with me, including ....

and ....

90.

The top three things I love that

you stand for are . . .

1.

2.

3.

91.

THE FUNNIEST THING YOU EVER SAID TO
ME IS ....

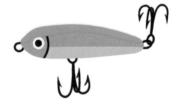

92.

You would be famous if the world knew how

good you are at ....

93.

I don't like the taste, but I love that you could

eat .... every day!

94.

_____ IS MY

FAVORITE THING WE EVER DID TOGETHER.

95.

I know that you love me by the way you

....

96.

You taught me to notice and care about the tiny

details, like .... and

.... , when you told

me ....

97.

I respect the way you ....

98.

I HOPE I MADE YOU PROUD

WHEN I ....

99.

There are still memories to be made together!

I still want to .... and

.... with you!

"extra love"

100.

I am who I am today because of your

. . . .

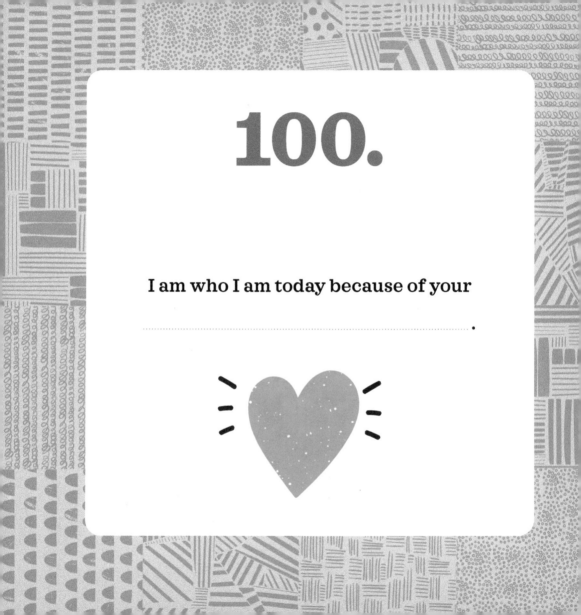